BADASS AFFIRMATIONS
Habit Tracker

Also by Becca Anderson

Badass Affirmations

Badass Advice

Positively Badass

Your Work from Home Life

Affirm Your Life

The Joy of Self-Care

Real Life Mindfulness

You Are an Awesome Woman

The Book of Awesome Women

BADASS AFFIRMATIONS

Habit Tracker

Your Daily Guide to Achieving Your Goals and Completing Your Tasks

Becca Anderson

Coral Gables

Published by Mango Publishing, a division of Mango Publishing Group, Inc.

Cover Design: Jermaine Lau

Illustrations: Jermaine Lau and Knstart Studio

Layout & Design: Jermaine Lau

For permission requests, please contact the publisher at:

Mango Publishing Group

2850 S Douglas Road, 2nd Floor

Coral Gables, FL 33134 USA

info@mango.bz

For special orders, quantity sales, course adoptions, and corporate sales, please email the publisher at sales@mango.bz. For trade and wholesale sales, please contact Ingram Publisher Services at customer.service@ingramcontent.com or +1.800.509.4887.

Badass Affirmations Habit Tracker: Your Daily Guide to Achieving Your Goals and Completing Your Tasks

ISBN: (p) 978-1-68481-201-1 (e) 978-1-68481-202-8

BISAC category code: SEL035000, SELF-HELP / Self-Management / Time Management

Table of Contents

Introduction

Badass Self-Care Is the Key to an Exceptional Life

This awesomely affirming habit tracker will help you plan for world domination, success in your life, and, most importantly, taking really good care of yourself.

You have to start with tending yourself—if you are worn down, depleted, or frazzled, you can't thrive, let alone enjoy your own life. Women especially often fall into the habit of what I call "putting yourself at the back of your own bus." You put your partner, your kids, your job, and your friends first. Well, actually...maybe your pets come ahead of the husband. The point is you take care of everyone else's needs first and, once you're done with all that, you don't have the energy to do much for yourself.

Please don't wear yourself out and put your own needs on the back burner. If you are completely depleted, you can't be at your peak in any area of life.

If you are at your *best*, you will actually make your loved ones (even the dog) happier, because they see you smiling, flowing, and looking good. A happy you is better for everyone! You will be more fine and have more fun when you are rocking the self-care.

Chapter 1

The Art of Affirmation

If you're anything like me, there are always aspects of your life or your personality that you're working to improve. After all, nobody's perfect—that's part of the beauty of life. We all make mistakes, we all have flawed habits, we all make unwise choices sometimes, and that's okay. In fact, that's great! But if you do want to continue learning and improving, it's probably not a smart idea to keep doing the same things you've been doing for years. It's time to try something new.

This is where affirmations come in. Affirmations are positive statements that you say out loud every day to help you shift your mindset in a positive and productive way. These statements can be about literally anything. For example, if you are trying to increase your self-confidence, you could say something like, "My self-confidence increases every day." Or if, let's say, you just had a difficult breakup and you're trying to shift your focus from your dating life (or lack thereof) to your career, then you could say to yourself, "I will focus on improving my job prospects," or "I am completely focused on my work." It's all about what changes you want to make in your mindset and, ultimately, your life.

Now, one of the main benefits of affirmations is that they help you to change how you think over time. You won't wake up one morning, say to yourself that you're going to be happy from now on, and then have the best day of your life every day until you die. (Well, you probably won't anyway, although I suppose anything is possible.) However, if you commit to taking five minutes of your morning to stand in front of the mirror, look yourself in the eye, and tell yourself that you are a beautiful, capable person who will achieve all you are working for, you'll find that, after a couple of weeks, you're actually starting to believe your own words. Maybe you'll stop cringing every time you look in the mirror, or maybe you'll start to notice all of the small steps you're making toward your big goals—the steps that have been made easier now that you know, and I mean *really* know, that you're capable of anything you set your mind to.

Affirmations aren't magic spells. You can't just *say* that you're eager to advance in your career and sit in your chair staring at a blank computer screen every day—you have to work your ass off and take advantage of the chance opportunities that come around. You can't just tell yourself that you're going to love your family members better and then proceed to ignore them every time they come near—you have to actually listen when they talk and respond patiently and kindly. What I'm saying is, if you don't follow up on your affirmations with actions, not much in your life will really change. I mean, it makes sense. Empty words are useless. But affirmations *are* the first step to a better morning, an improved mindset, and a version of you that is more confident and focused.

Badass Practice

Write Your Own Affirmations

As you create your own affirmations, remember that they must be positive and personal. Make sure to use the present tense. See some examples below:

AFFIRMATION STATION

I am confident. I am strong. I am powerful.

Write your own affirmations below:

DATE

Weekly Objectives:

AFFIRMATION STATION

HABIT	MON	TUES	WED	THURS	FRI	SAT	SUN
Drink twelve cups of water							
Move/exercise							
Eat all three meals							
Check in with friends or family							
Sleep well							
Practice hobby/interest							
Reflect on your day							

DATE

Monday

Tuesday

Wednesday

Thursday

Tasks	Date

Friday

Saturday

Sunday

Tasks	Date

Weekly Thoughts and Reflections

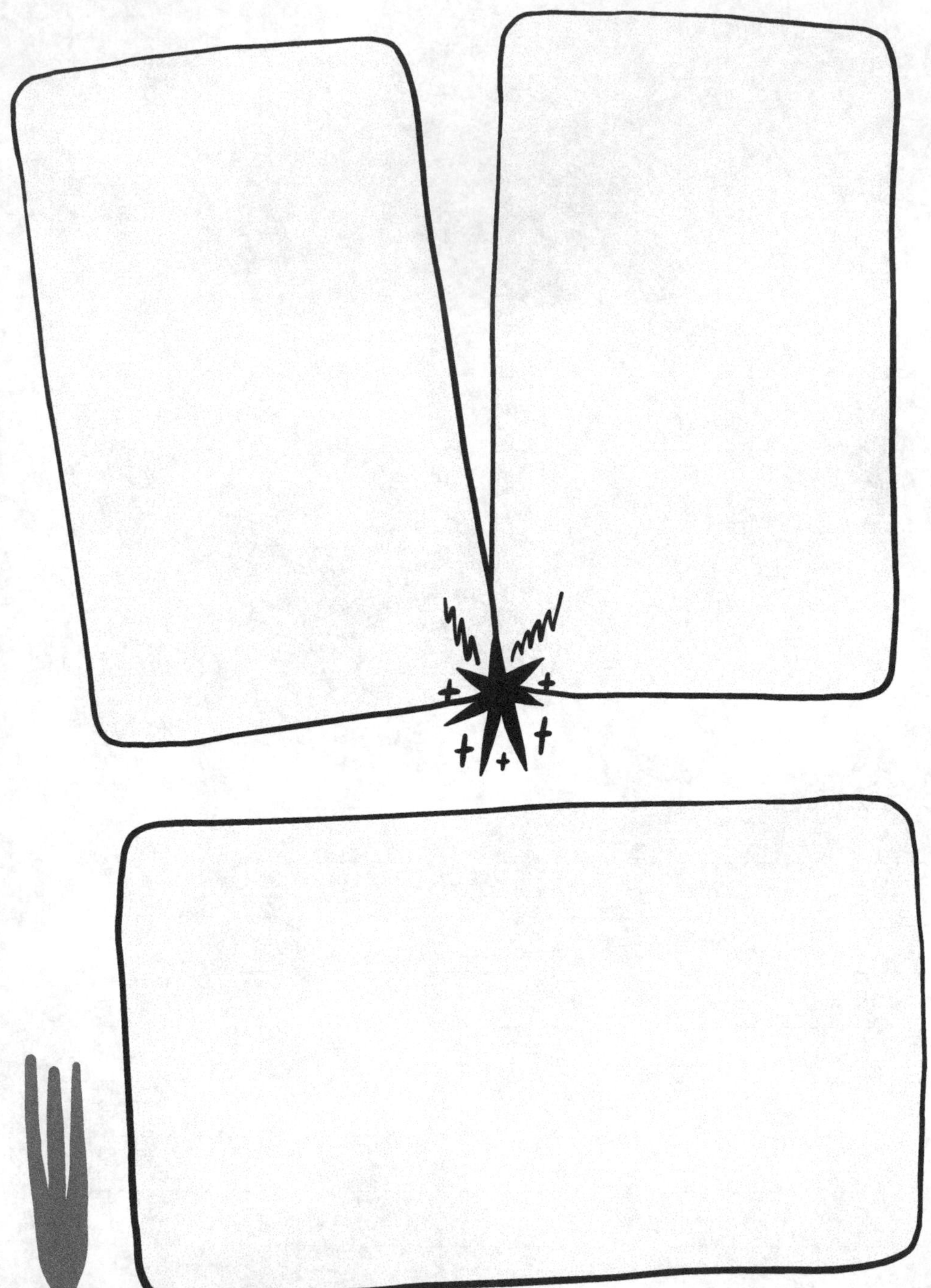

DATE

Weekly Objectives:

AFFIRMATION STATION

HABIT	MON	TUES	WED	THURS	FRI	SAT	SUN

DATE

Monday

Tuesday

Wednesday

Thursday

Tasks	Date

Friday

Saturday

Sunday

Tasks	Date

Weekly Thoughts and Reflections

DATE

Weekly Objectives:

AFFIRMATION STATION

HABIT	MON	TUES	WED	THURS	FRI	SAT	SUN

DATE

Monday

Tuesday

Wednesday

Thursday

Tasks	Date

Friday

Saturday

Sunday

Tasks	Date

Weekly Thoughts and Reflections

DATE

Weekly Objectives:

AFFIRMATION STATION

HABIT	MON	TUES	WED	THURS	FRI	SAT	SUN

DATE

Monday

Tuesday

Wednesday

Thursday

Tasks	Date

Friday

Saturday

Sunday

Tasks	Date

Weekly Thoughts and Reflections

Chapter 2

Visualize It! Intend It!

Wellness is a topic on nearly everyone's minds these days. We've learned that a life lived at breakneck speed comes to a screeching halt when we hit burnout or face a crisis. The purpose of this habit tracker is to make sure you never hit that wall and that your life is lived at a very human pace, filled with joy and work you love and take pride in. Your life needs to have room for *you*. Lots of it.

Thankfully, we humans are a resilient lot. By managing your time, you can enjoy cooking nutritious meals, meditating, and taking long walks in the park and neighborhood, which have become healthy new habits embraced by many. I highly recommend you pry yourself away from work and your laptop to discover the true rapture of gardening, along with brewing herbal teas, cooking fresh homegrown veggies, and all the simple pleasures of a slow-paced lifestyle. Slowing down and establishing healthier habits will create a happier you! Setting an intention for your day is a good place to start.

To achieve lifelong well-being, you need to bring this practice to every day of your life. Regular rituals will go a long way to making visualization and intention second nature to you. Every single morning, before I even open my eyes, I set an intention for my day. I visualize how it is going to go and state aloud my intention for it to turn out really well. I then state aloud my vision for the day. This practice takes only a few moments and sets a positive tone for my day. Because I set a daily intention, I begin each day calm, grounded, and centered. Your intentions are just for you—it should be what works for you. Below is an example of a recent intention of mine, which I hope can serve as an encouragement to you. And I intend this to work extremely well for you!

Badass Practice

Daily Morning Intention

"I intend today's writing to flow easily, to be filled with inspiration that helps people and fills their hearts with happiness."

Now set your own intention!

1. State your intention.
2. When you decide what you want, vocalize it or write it down.
3. Be clear. Make sure your intention is positive.
4. Keep your intention simple.
5. Shift any limiting beliefs.

Set your intentions below:

DATE

Weekly Objectives:

AFFIRMATION STATION

HABIT	MON	TUES	WED	THURS	FRI	SAT	SUN
Drink twelve cups of water							
Move/exercise							
Eat all three meals							
Check in with friends or family							
Sleep well							
Practice hobby/interest							
Reflect on your day							

DATE

Monday

Tuesday

Wednesday

Thursday

Tasks	Date

Friday

Saturday

Sunday

Tasks	Date

Weekly Thoughts and Reflections

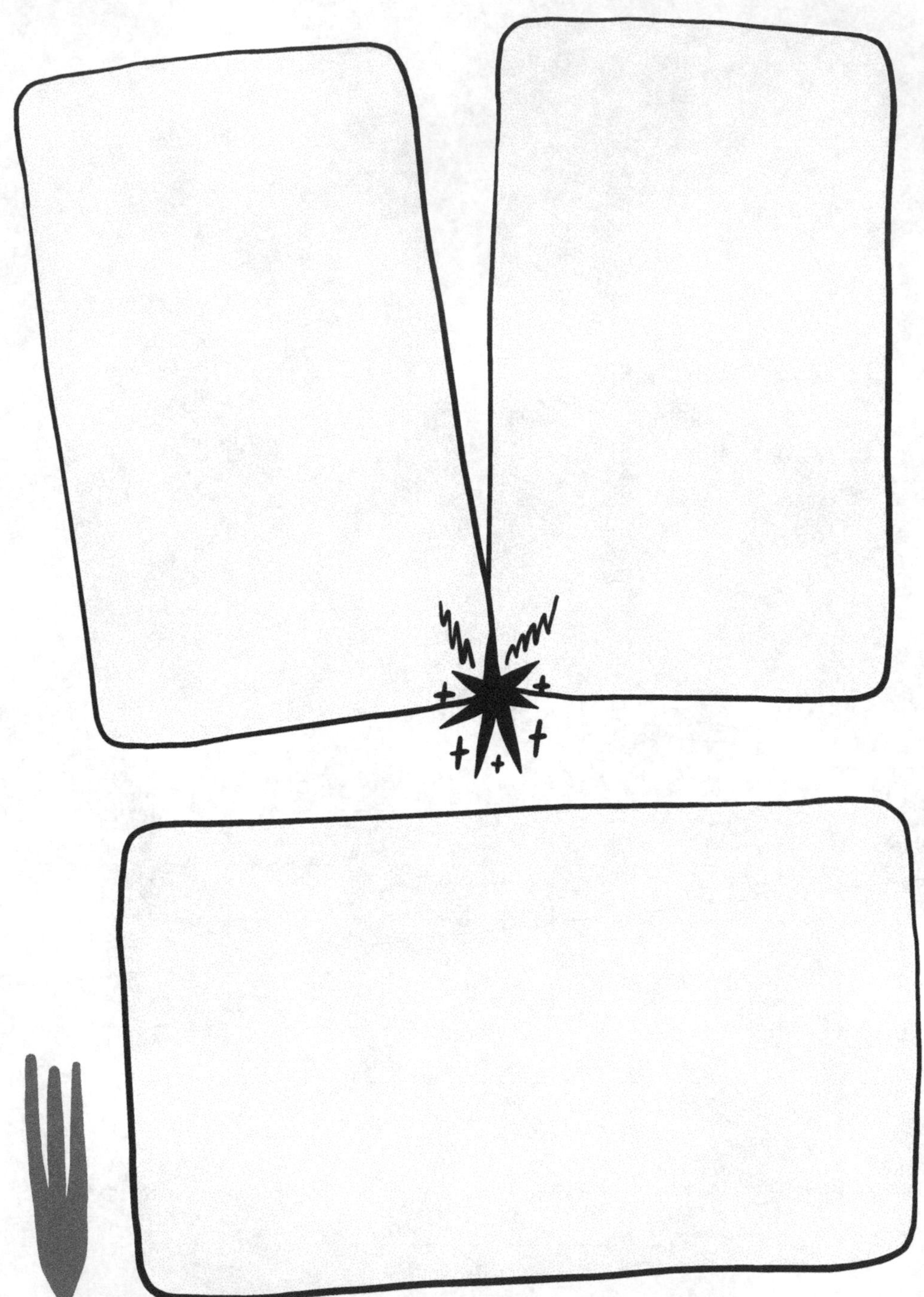

DATE

Weekly Objectives:

AFFIRMATION STATION

HABIT	MON	TUES	WED	THURS	FRI	SAT	SUN

DATE

Monday

Tuesday

Wednesday

Thursday

Tasks	Date

Friday

Saturday

Sunday

Tasks	Date

Weekly Thoughts and Reflections

DATE

Weekly Objectives:

AFFIRMATION STATION

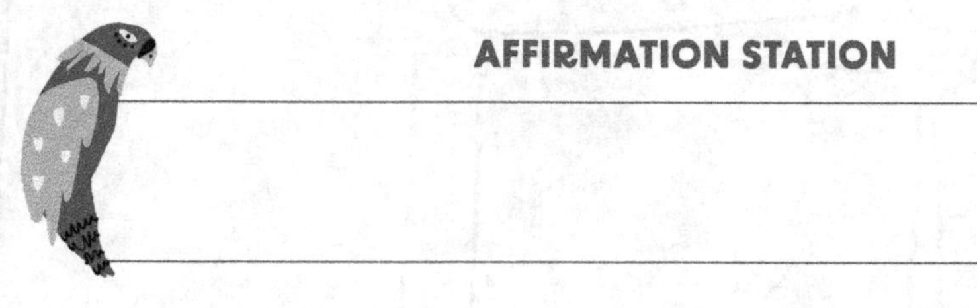

HABIT	MON	TUES	WED	THURS	FRI	SAT	SUN

DATE

Monday

Tuesday

Wednesday

Thursday

Tasks	Date

Friday

Saturday

Sunday

Tasks	Date

Weekly Thoughts and Reflections

DATE

Weekly Objectives:

AFFIRMATION STATION

HABIT	MON	TUES	WED	THURS	FRI	SAT	SUN

DATE

Monday

Tuesday

Wednesday

Thursday

Tasks	Date

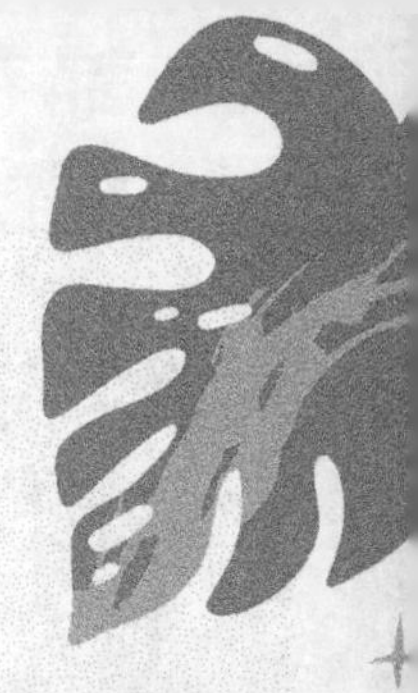

Friday

Saturday

Sunday

Tasks	Date

Weekly Thoughts and Reflections

Chapter 3

Natural Healing—Movement and the Great Outdoors

When you wake up each morning, what comes first into your mind? Ideally, it is a sense of the possible and of your vibrant life. And, indeed, every day is alive with possibility. Every single day is a good day to be alive on this abundant planet that gives us everything we need: air, water, heat, the outdoors, and all the good things that come from it. Holding an awareness of this origin will keep you conscious of yourself, your breath, your energy levels, and how you feel in your body. As you wake up every day, you should connect to your body and breathe each new day in (this is a perfect time to set your intention as well).

If you are an early riser, all the better, as the dew of dawn is beneficial to your health. I learned this from a grandmother who did a bit of tai chi every morning in her backyard and lived to be 108, which she attributed to this practice (though I know she also drank many pots of herbal tea).

What I suggest you do is find the daily rituals that are soothing to you in body, mind, and soul. Like the Chinese grandmother, you should breathe, move, and awaken into your day with awareness and mindfulness. You won't find and implement the meditations, prayers, and practices that make you feel grounded and whole overnight; this process can and should take time. What really nurtures you? What really quiets your mind and fills you with peace and positivity? Find these approaches to sacred care and journal about your progress as you discover what feeds you, as you listen deeply to your heart.

Badass Practice

Get Grounded, Literally

I love that earth is coming into vogue as more and more people realize the need to spend time with nature. You don't need to go to a mountaintop to get in touch with Mother Earth; try your own backyard, explore a nearby park, or visit a friend's farm. Whichever you choose, make sure it is a dry, sunny, and warm day. Just take yourself and a blanket. Find a place that looks right to you and that you are drawn to and set your blanket and any belongings down, so you are holding nothing. Remove your shoes and stand on the earth itself. Wiggle your toes to feel the soil underneath you. Feel free to spend as much time as you like in your earthing space. Commune with nature safely in the embrace of Mother Earth.

Write down when and where you plan to practice earthing here:

DATE

Weekly Objectives:

AFFIRMATION STATION

HABIT	MON	TUES	WED	THURS	FRI	SAT	SUN
Drink twelve cups of water							
Move/exercise							
Eat all three meals							
Check in with friends or family							
Sleep well							
Practice hobby/interest							
Reflect on your day							

DATE

Monday

Tuesday

Wednesday

Thursday

Tasks	Date

Friday

Saturday

Sunday

Tasks	Date

Weekly Thoughts and Reflections

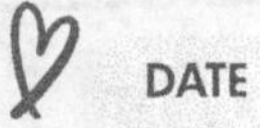

DATE

Weekly Objectives:

AFFIRMATION STATION

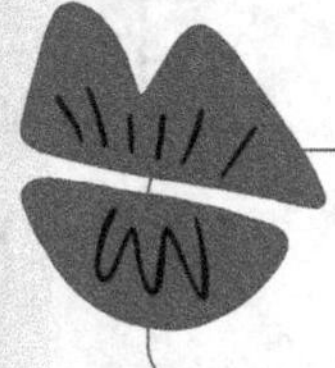

HABIT	MON	TUES	WED	THURS	FRI	SAT	SUN

DATE

Monday

Tuesday

Wednesday

Thursday

Tasks	Date

Friday

Saturday

Sunday

Tasks	Date

Weekly Thoughts and Reflections

DATE

Weekly Objectives:

AFFIRMATION STATION

HABIT	MON	TUES	WED	THURS	FRI	SAT	SUN

DATE

Monday

Tuesday

Wednesday

Thursday

Tasks	Date

Friday

Saturday

Sunday

Tasks	Date

Weekly Thoughts and Reflections

DATE

Weekly Objectives:

AFFIRMATION STATION

HABIT	MON	TUES	WED	THURS	FRI	SAT	SUN

DATE

Monday

Tuesday

Wednesday

Thursday

Tasks	Date

Friday

Saturday

Sunday

Tasks	Date

Weekly Thoughts and Reflections

DATE

Weekly Objectives:

AFFIRMATION STATION

DATE

Monday

Tuesday

Wednesday

Thursday

Tasks	Date

Friday

Saturday

Sunday

Tasks	Date

Weekly Thoughts and Reflections

Chapter 4

Acts of Kindness (Be Kind to Yourself Too)

I am very blessed to have been part of the team that brought *Random Acts of Kindness* to the world. It was a highlight of my career and imprinted in/on me the power of the human heart. Acts of kindness can be large or small, but they are a wonderful thing to incorporate into your life by adopting a kind mindset.

Get acquainted with simple human kindness and easy acts of goodness every day. When at the grocery store, return your shopping cart or help the elderly man struggling with his bags. Open doors for people. Say "Hello" with a smile. Every day, and in every way, choose to take the high road in your travels. The view is much more beautiful from up top!

But don't forget to be kind to yourself!

Make a commitment to refrain from negative self-talk. Be kind to yourself and focus on the traits you like, rather than the ones you don't. The extremely wise Dawna Markova, the author of *I Will Not Die an Unlived Life* (a favorite book of mine), says, "Your soul remembers when you put yourself down; it imprints upon you. Never do this. Self-compassion is key to a life well-lived."

INSTANT KINDNESS: LOOK UP!

Put down your smartphone and make eye contact, person to person. Nowadays, I consider that a major act of kindness, and courtesy as well.

Badass Practice

DIY Optimism

Try this easy way to craft some kindness. Make a sign that reads, "Take what you need," with tear-off tabs on the bottom that say, "love," "courage," "optimism," and so on. Hang it up in places you regularly pass by. Keep refills at the ready!

What are some other acts of kindness, for either yourself or others, you can incorporate into your daily life?

DATE

Weekly Objectives:

AFFIRMATION STATION

HABIT	MON	TUES	WED	THURS	FRI	SAT	SUN
Drink twelve cups of water							
Move/exercise							
Eat all three meals							
Check in with friends or family							
Sleep well							
Practice hobby/interest							
Reflect on your day							

DATE

Monday

Tuesday

Wednesday

Thursday

Tasks	Date

Friday

Saturday

Sunday

Tasks	Date

Weekly Thoughts and Reflections

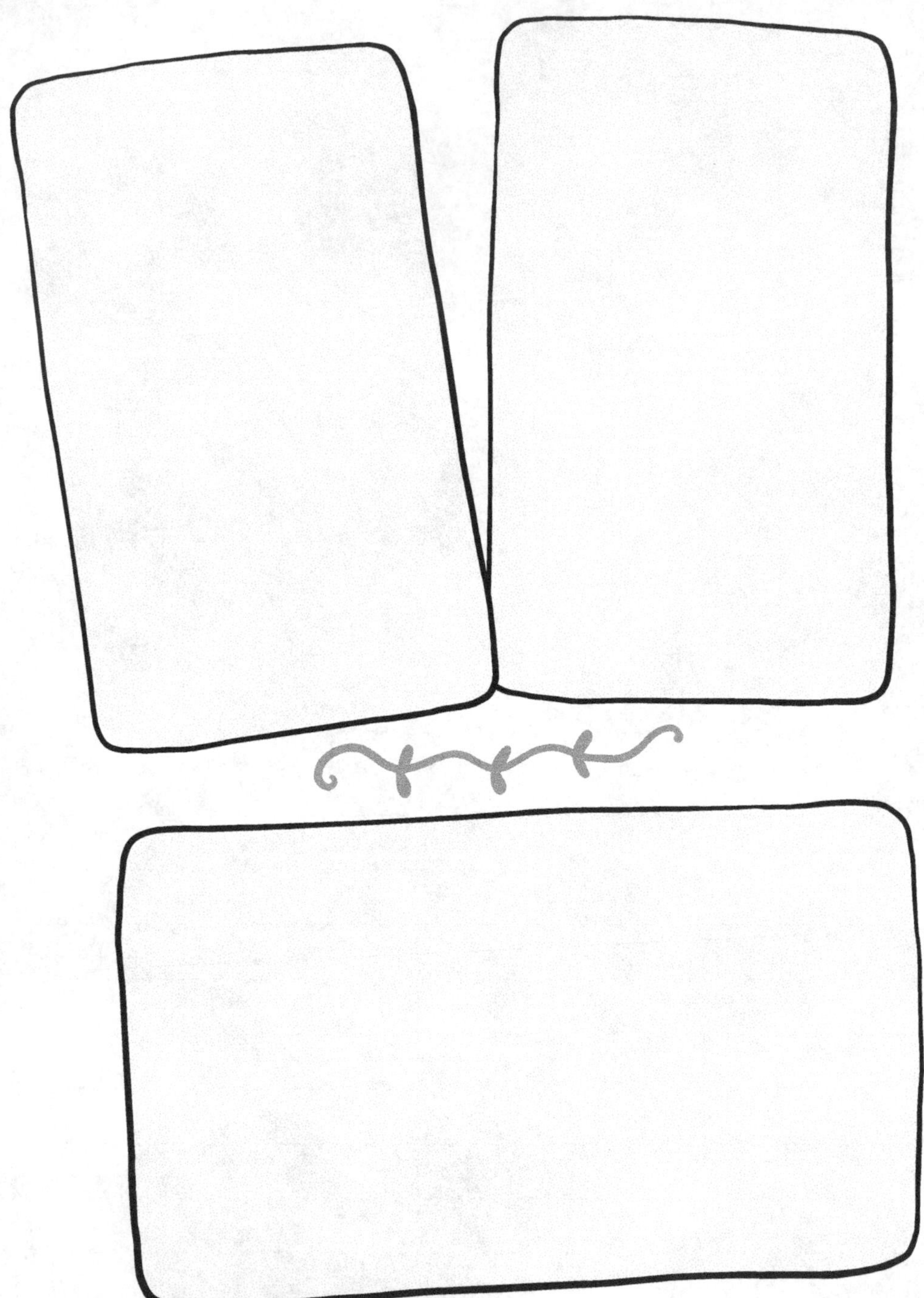

DATE

Weekly Objectives:

AFFIRMATION STATION

HABIT	MON	TUES	WED	THURS	FRI	SAT	SUN

DATE

Monday

Tuesday

Wednesday

Thursday

Tasks	Date

Friday

Saturday

Sunday

Tasks	Date

Weekly Thoughts and Reflections

DATE

Weekly Objectives:

AFFIRMATION STATION

HABIT	MON	TUES	WED	THURS	FRI	SAT	SUN

DATE

Monday

Tuesday

Wednesday

Thursday

Tasks	Date

Friday

Saturday

Sunday

Tasks	Date

Weekly Thoughts and Reflections

DATE

Weekly Objectives:

AFFIRMATION STATION

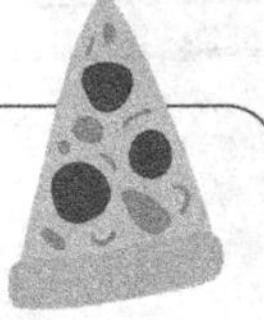

HABIT	MON	TUES	WED	THURS	FRI	SAT	SUN

DATE

Monday

Tuesday

Wednesday

Thursday

Tasks	Date

Friday

Saturday

Sunday

Tasks	Date

Weekly Thoughts and Reflections

Chapter 5

Badass Brilliance Habits—You Can Do All Things (with Enough Self-Belief)

This is your life! Only you can truly control your choices. Choosing happiness is the most effective way to be good to yourself as well as to the world. Here are some suggestions for how you can ensure simple joy in your life:

- Be the best you can be by your own standards
- Surround yourself with people who inspire you and make you feel good
- Focus on what you have, not what you lack
- Remember that optimism trumps pessimism every time!
- Smile often and genuinely
- Be honest, with yourself and others
- Help others
- Embrace your past, live in the present, and look forward for what is yet to come

REWIRE YOUR BRAIN TO BE MORE POSITIVE

Neuropsychiatrist David Amen, MD, posits that thoughts carry physical properties and that the properties of negative thoughts can be detrimental to leading a healthy, happy life. To overcome these negative effects, he prescribes thinking more positively to change the way your brain works and, in turn, change your life for the better.

Now, what are you going to do with your newfound supersmart positivity?

Badass Practice

Add a Half Hour to Your Day

This is one of the most brilliantly simple pieces of advice and one of my all-time best "life hacks." Wake up a half hour earlier each day, and use these thirty minutes to reach out to people. It can be as easy as wishing a happy birthday to your Facebook contacts, making one meaningful phone call first thing in the morning, or writing a personal note to someone you have been meaning to be in contact with. I remember thinking I really didn't want to get up any earlier; my days were long enough. But this slight change has been absolutely transformative. It is a kind of self-care too, because it lifts my heart and spirit as few other things can do. The extra half hour of every morning has been one of the most valuable investments I have ever made—so much so that I made it an hour. It completely changed my life for the better. Try it!

Make a list below of what you'll do with that extra half hour this week:

DATE

Weekly Objectives:

AFFIRMATION STATION

HABIT	MON	TUES	WED	THURS	FRI	SAT	SUN
Drink twelve cups of water							
Move/exercise							
Eat all three meals							
Check in with friends or family							
Sleep well							
Practice hobby/interest							
Reflect on your day							

DATE

Monday

Tuesday

Wednesday

Thursday

Tasks	Date

Friday

Saturday

Sunday

Tasks	Date

Weekly Thoughts and Reflections

DATE

Weekly Objectives:

AFFIRMATION STATION

HABIT	MON	TUES	WED	THURS	FRI	SAT	SUN

DATE

Monday

Tuesday

Wednesday

Thursday

Tasks	Date

Friday

Saturday

Sunday

Tasks	Date

Weekly Thoughts and Reflections

DATE

Weekly Objectives:

AFFIRMATION STATION

HABIT	MON	TUES	WED	THURS	FRI	SAT	SUN

DATE

Monday

Tuesday

Wednesday

Thursday

Tasks	Date

Friday

Saturday

Sunday

Tasks	Date

Weekly Thoughts and Reflections

DATE

Weekly Objectives:

AFFIRMATION STATION

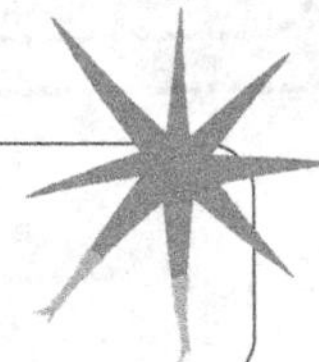

HABIT	MON	TUES	WED	THURS	FRI	SAT	SUN

DATE

Monday

Tuesday

Wednesday

Thursday

Tasks	Date

Friday

Saturday

Sunday

Tasks	Date

Weekly Thoughts and Reflections

DATE

Weekly Objectives:

AFFIRMATION STATION

HABIT	MON	TUES	WED	THURS	FRI	SAT	SUN

DATE

Monday

Tuesday

Wednesday

Thursday

Tasks	Date

Friday

Saturday

Sunday

Tasks	Date

Weekly Thoughts and Reflections

Chapter 6

Unplug and Recharge Your Own Battery

So many of us are tethered to our devices, whether it is smartphones, tablets, or even Fitbits or watches that track every moment of our lives and remind us about meetings, appointments, and other "emergencies" with chimes and all manner of alarms. We all have so much going on! Maybe too much. Here is a very simple and effective badass habit: unplug!

Pick a day and don't use any technological devices. Texting, checking your Twitter feed, watching your favorite YouTube videos, and checking your email all can wait until tomorrow! Turn off your devices and turn on your senses! Read a book, cook a meal, and enjoy the outdoors by taking a walk or tending to your garden. Technology distracts us from the real world, occupying our attention with games, chat rooms, social media websites, commercials, and so on. Want to know what's going on in the news? Read a newspaper. Be aware of the here and now by finding activities that don't require electricity or a battery. Make your own entertainment.

Badass Practice

Your Goals Will Grow You

Make a list of short-term goals you would like to achieve by the end of the year, month, or even week. I find it's easier to think of these goals at the end of a tech-free day. As you accomplish these goals, give gratitude for the hard work, inspiration, people, and other factors that helped you along the way. My goal is to give more to those around me, near and far. I would love to hear yours!

Write down some of your short-term goals below:

DATE

Weekly Objectives:

AFFIRMATION STATION

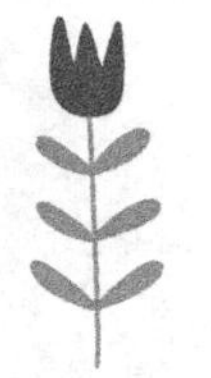

HABIT	MON	TUES	WED	THURS	FRI	SAT	SUN
Drink twelve cups of water							
Move/exercise							
Eat all three meals							
Check in with friends or family							
Sleep well							
Practice hobby/interest							
Reflect on your day							

DATE

Monday

Tuesday

Wednesday

Thursday

Tasks	Date

Friday

Saturday

Sunday

Tasks	Date

Weekly Thoughts and Reflections

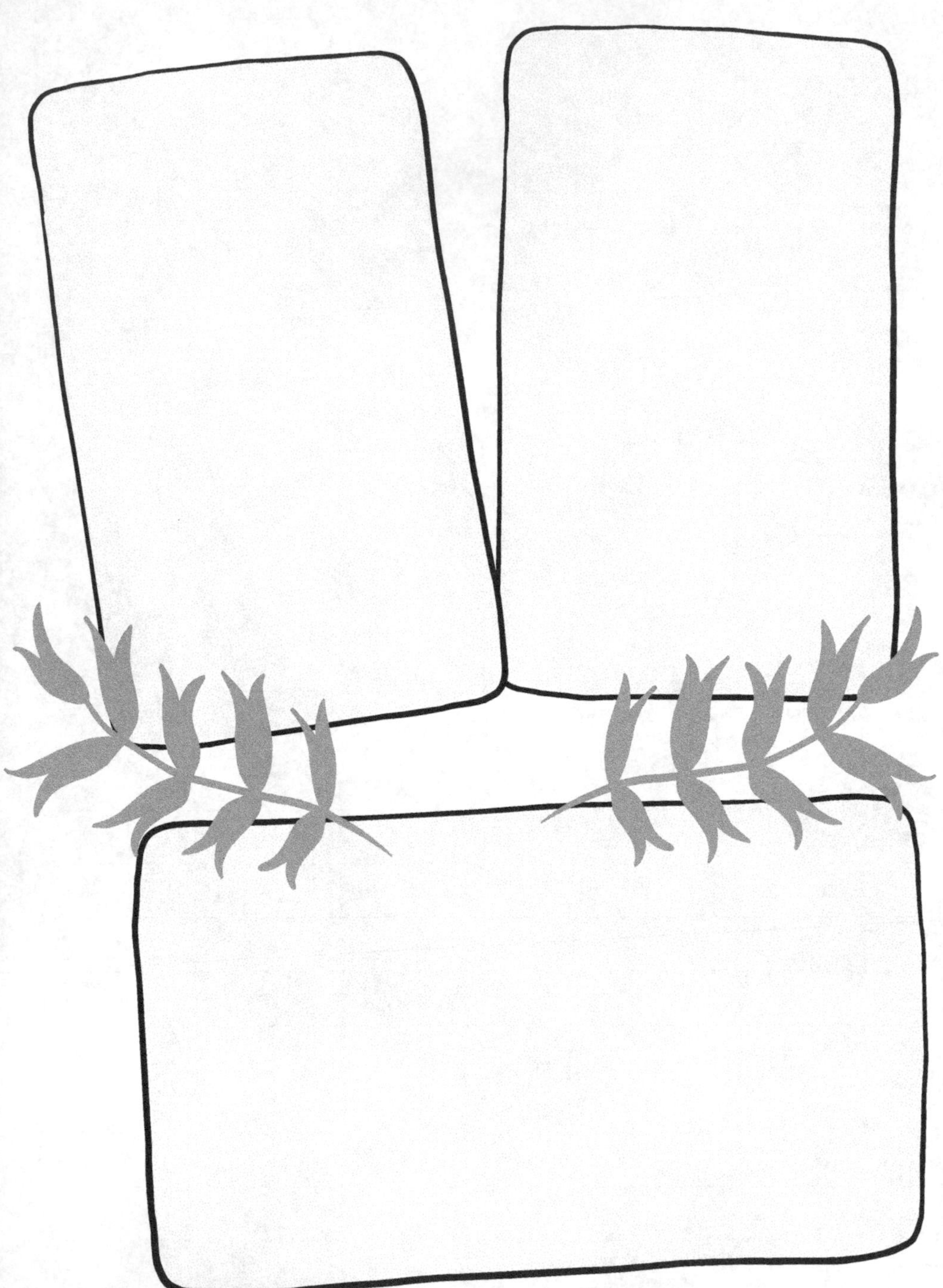

DATE

Weekly Objectives:

AFFIRMATION STATION

HABIT	MON	TUES	WED	THURS	FRI	SAT	SUN

DATE

Monday

Tuesday

Wednesday

Thursday

Tasks	Date

Friday

Saturday

Sunday

Tasks	Date

Weekly Thoughts and Reflections

DATE

Weekly Objectives:

AFFIRMATION STATION

DATE

Monday

Tuesday

Wednesday

Thursday

Tasks	Date

Friday

Saturday

Sunday

Tasks	Date

Weekly Thoughts and Reflections

DATE

Weekly Objectives:

AFFIRMATION STATION

HABIT	MON	TUES	WED	THURS	FRI	SAT	SUN

DATE

Monday

Tuesday

Wednesday

Thursday

Tasks	Date

Friday

Saturday

Sunday

Tasks	Date

Weekly Thoughts and Reflections

Chapter 7

We Are Here to Love 24/7, 365 Days a Year

A few years ago, I had a major epiphany after struggling through a period of great difficulty. I have always worked hard and, like all of us, had my ambitions. After this hardship, I suddenly realized that the only thing that matters is how much love you give over the course of your life. Consider this: what regrets might you face on your deathbed? I have read a good bit on this, including what doctors and nurses hear so often, and it has nothing to do with how much money you have, your performance reviews at work, or other "worldly" concerns. Surely you will think about your loved ones—did you tell them how much you love them? Did you show your true heart to others? Did you give enough of yourself in your life? I'm confident that is the only thing that will matter. Telling people how you feel is very, very important. Tell everyone you love how much you love them as often as possible!

Badass Practice

Love the Ones You're With

I have seen this excellent exercise put into practice at work, family reunions, and dinner parties. It never fails to bring a group of people closer, and it brings out the best in everyone. Call everyone to attention and say you want to acknowledge your appreciation for the group. Time your moment well—whenever there is a lull in conversation would be best and never at the beginning of a get-together.

Here are some examples:

- "What I appreciate about Julian is his humility; he is brilliant but never showy."
- "What I appreciate about Leslie is her kindness and generosity. She helped me out when I was in a bad way. I will always be grateful to her for that."

Offer a positive appreciation for each person and encourage others to do the same. Talk about a turnaround! This can turn stormy skies blue in five minutes flat.

Write the names of some people who deserve your appreciation, and check them off once you've expressed it to them:

DATE

Weekly Objectives:

AFFIRMATION STATION

HABIT	MON	TUES	WED	THURS	FRI	SAT	SUN
Drink twelve cups of water							
Move/exercise							
Eat all three meals							
Check in with friends or family							
Sleep well							
Practice hobby/interest							
Reflect on your day							

DATE

Monday

Tuesday

Wednesday

Thursday

Tasks	Date

Friday

Saturday

Sunday

Tasks	Date

Weekly Thoughts and Reflections

DATE

Weekly Objectives:

AFFIRMATION STATION

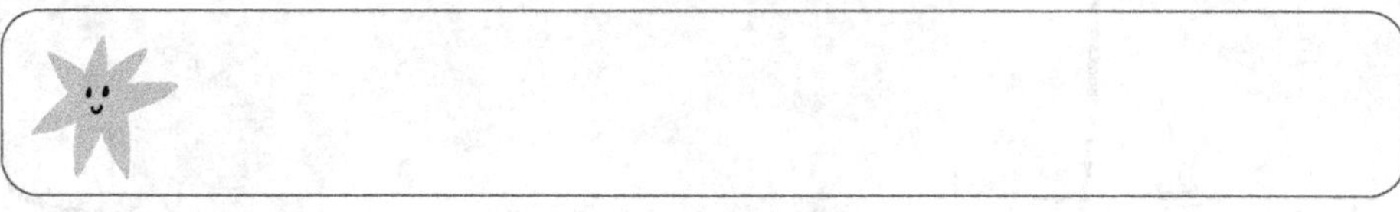

HABIT	MON	TUES	WED	THURS	FRI	SAT	SUN

DATE

Monday

Tuesday

Wednesday

Thursday

Tasks	Date

Friday

Saturday

Sunday

Tasks	Date

Weekly Thoughts and Reflections

DATE

Weekly Objectives:

AFFIRMATION STATION

HABIT	MON	TUES	WED	THURS	FRI	SAT	SUN

DATE

Monday

Tuesday

Wednesday

Thursday

Tasks	Date

Friday

Saturday

Sunday

Tasks	Date

DATE

Weekly Objectives:

AFFIRMATION STATION

HABIT	MON	TUES	WED	THURS	FRI	SAT	SUN

DATE

Monday

Tuesday

Wednesday

Thursday

Tasks	Date

Friday

Saturday

Sunday

Tasks	Date

Weekly Thoughts and Reflections

Chapter 8

Meditation Makes You Smarter (and Way Calmer!)

Did you know that having a regular mindfulness practice is not just good for your soul and your body but is *fantastic* for your brain? It's true! Meditation creates new neural pathways which keep you sharp, can prevent memory issues later in life, helps you fend off depression, and boosts your self-esteem. There is oodles of research on this fabulous fact, and Johns Hopkins has some very impressive studies on this.

Meditation doesn't have to be boring, and you don't need to be sitting in a lotus position on the floor. It can be very active and include movement.

Try getting out of your head and into your heart.

Because the world we exist in today is very much about staying in our heads, many of us have to make a concentrated effort to become grounded and in touch with our bodies and the natural world around us. Grounding is a technique for centering yourself within your being. It is a way we can reconnect and balance ourselves through the power of the Earth's elements. When you see someone driving past, talking on their cell phone, you know that they are not grounded.

For deep grounding, try creative visualization or, better yet, a group guided meditation.

Badass Practice

A Walking Meditation with Benefits

This is the simplest of rituals: one you can do every day of your life. Go for a walk and, as you stroll, take the time to look and really see what is in your path. For example, my friend Eileen takes a bag with her and picks up pieces of what she calls "future recycling" in her path. She does this as an act of love for the earth. During the ten years she practiced this walking meditation, she has probably turned a mountain of garbage into recycled glass, paper, and plastic. Eileen is *very* grounded. She is also a deeply happy person who shares joy with all in her path.

Write below when and where you will go on your next walking meditation:

DATE

Weekly Objectives:

AFFIRMATION STATION

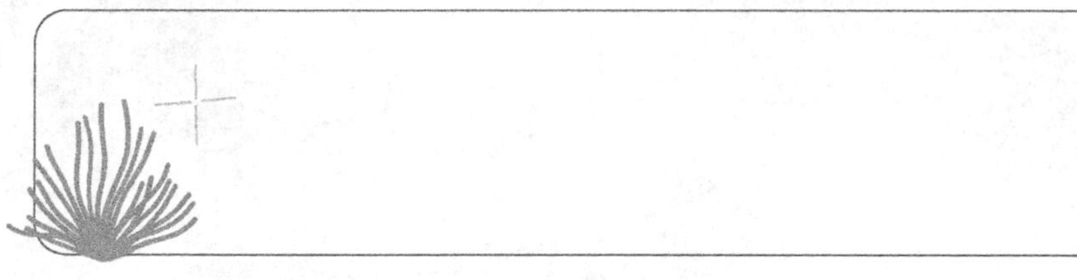

HABIT	MON	TUES	WED	THURS	FRI	SAT	SUN
Drink twelve cups of water							
Move/exercise							
Eat all three meals							
Check in with friends or family							
Sleep well							
Practice hobby/interest							
Reflect on your day							

DATE

Monday

Tuesday

Wednesday

Thursday

Tasks	Date

Friday

Saturday

Sunday

Tasks	Date

Weekly Thoughts and Reflections

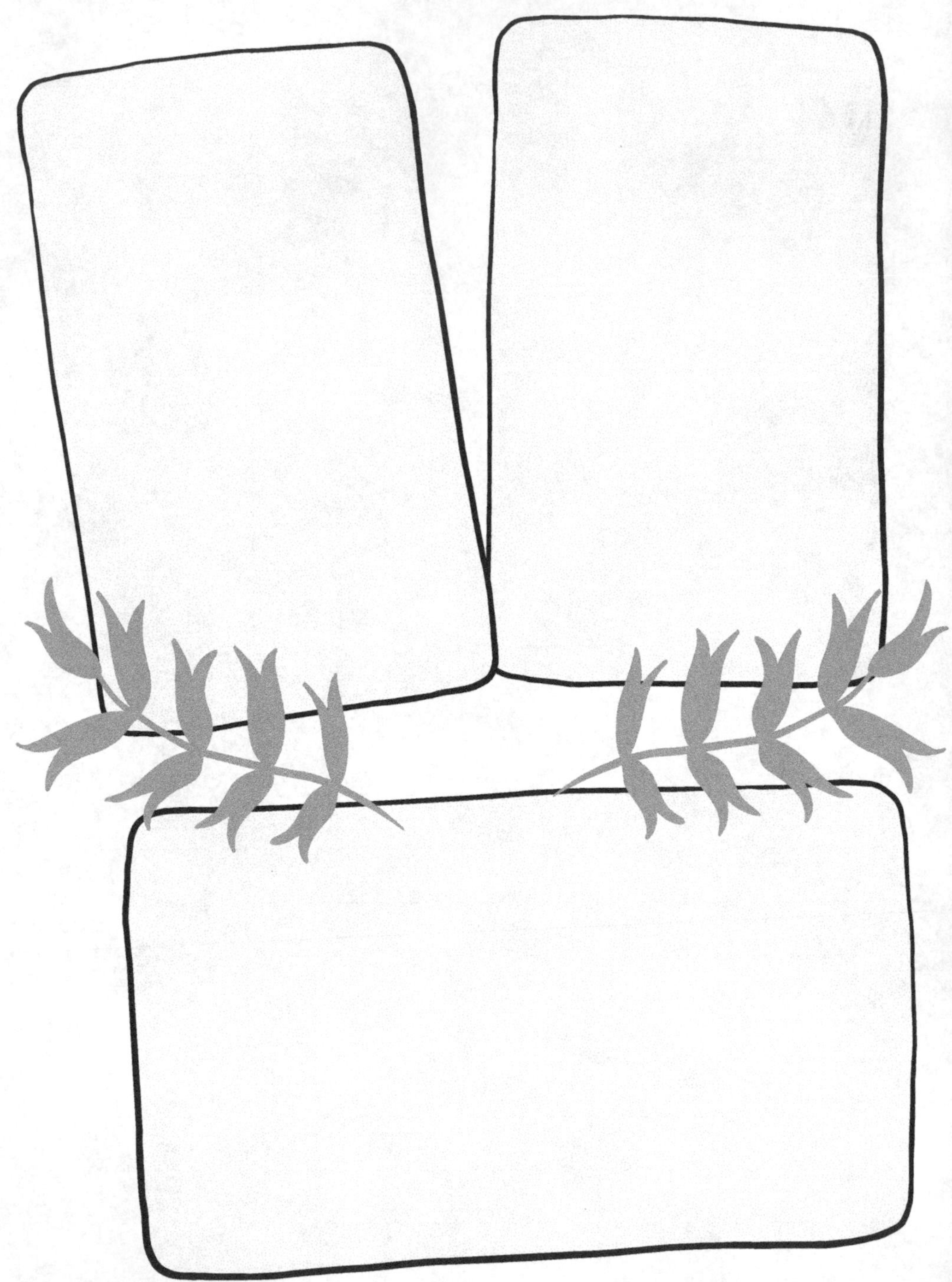

DATE

Weekly Objectives:

AFFIRMATION STATION

HABIT	MON	TUES	WED	THURS	FRI	SAT	SUN

DATE

Monday

Tuesday

Wednesday

Thursday

Tasks	Date

Friday

Saturday

Sunday

Tasks	Date

Weekly Thoughts and Reflections

DATE

Weekly Objectives:

AFFIRMATION STATION

HABIT	MON	TUES	WED	THURS	FRI	SAT	SUN

DATE

Monday

Tuesday

Wednesday

Thursday

Tasks	Date

Friday

Saturday

Sunday

Tasks

Date

Weekly Thoughts and Reflections

DATE

Weekly Objectives:

AFFIRMATION STATION

HABIT	MON	TUES	WED	THURS	FRI	SAT	SUN

DATE

Monday

Tuesday

Wednesday

Thursday

Tasks	Date

Friday

Saturday

Sunday

Tasks	Date

Weekly Thoughts and Reflections

 DATE

Weekly Objectives:

AFFIRMATION STATION

HABIT	MON	TUES	WED	THURS	FRI	SAT	SUN

DATE

Monday

Tuesday

Wednesday

Thursday

Tasks	Date

Friday

Saturday

Sunday

Tasks	Date

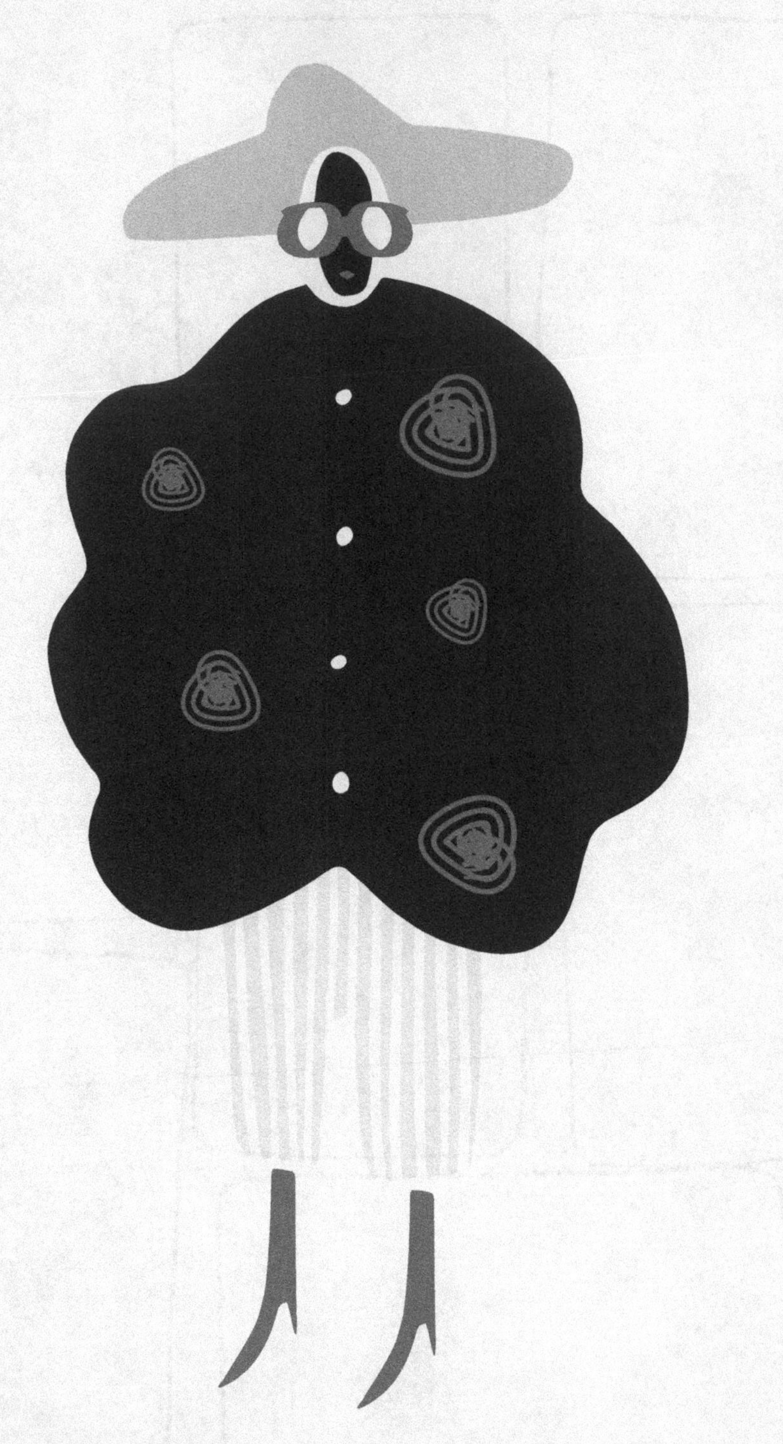

Chapter 9

Badass Inspiration—Face a Fear and Conquer It

I count myself as fortunate to not have many regrets. The ones I do have come from when I didn't try something. There was one time when I was too embarrassed to take up an instrument as an adult because I worried about how terrible I would sound; other times I didn't try a sport or join a group activity because I felt awkward. In hindsight, that all seems so silly to me. No one was judging me, except myself!

Let go of all that baggage and try new things. Learn as you go, and you will learn as you grow! I call this "Imagine a Day" where you think of something new and just do it!

Here is what I now know to be true: lack of imagination is the only limitation, and fear creates self-doubt. Take yourself out of "fear mode" and unlock the power of your own imagination. I urge you to imagine a day: pick something like painting, French cookery, playing piano, singing, learning a foreign language, yoga, rock-climbing, ballroom dancing, pottery, snorkeling—something that speaks to you on a profound level but scares you just a little. Find a class or experience and dive right in. Live your life no holds barred and regret free!

Badass Practice

List Your Life Dream

Instead of writing up and crossing things off of a bucket list, create a "life list." Let your hopes, dreams, fears, and thoughts spill out of you and onto this list. Next to each entry, write down how that emotion or fear makes you feel—does it hold you back or empower you? This task will put you on the road to self-discovery. Knowing who you are is important in order to have relationships with others. Know thyself.

Start the list below:

DATE

Weekly Objectives:

AFFIRMATION STATION

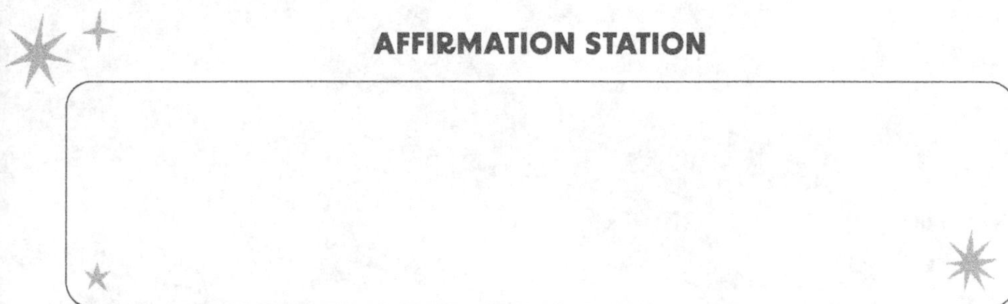

HABIT	MON	TUES	WED	THURS	FRI	SAT	SUN
Drink twelve cups of water							
Move/exercise							
Eat all three meals							
Check in with friends or family							
Sleep well							
Practice hobby/interest							
Reflect on your day							

DATE

Monday

Tuesday

Wednesday

Thursday

Tasks	Date

Friday

Saturday

Sunday

Tasks	Date

Weekly Thoughts and Reflections

DATE

Weekly Objectives:

AFFIRMATION STATION

HABIT	MON	TUES	WED	THURS	FRI	SAT	SUN

DATE

Monday

Tuesday

Wednesday

Thursday

Tasks	Date

Friday

Saturday

Sunday

Tasks	Date

Weekly Thoughts and Reflections

DATE

Weekly Objectives:

AFFIRMATION STATION

HABIT	MON	TUES	WED	THURS	FRI	SAT	SUN

DATE

Monday

Tuesday

Wednesday

Thursday

Tasks	Date

Friday

Saturday

Sunday

Tasks	Date

Weekly Thoughts and Reflections

DATE

Weekly Objectives:

AFFIRMATION STATION

HABIT	MON	TUES	WED	THURS	FRI	SAT	SUN

DATE

Monday

Tuesday

Wednesday

Thursday

Tasks	Date

Friday

Saturday

Sunday

Tasks	Date

Weekly Thoughts and Reflections

Chapter 10

Esteem Others as You Would Esteem Yourself

Compliment someone today and mean it. A genuine compliment can boost someone's confidence and that is a great feeling. If you like your coworker's blouse or new haircut (or both!), tell her. Open and honest communication works wonders for developing relationships and makes everybody's day a little bit nicer. You can change the trajectory of someone's day/week/month by simply asking them, "Do you know how great you are?"

CATCH PEOPLE DOING SOMETHING RIGHT (AND MAKE SURE THEY KNOW IT)

During difficult transitions, our natural tendency is to resist change and grow rigid. In this state, we seem to only be able to focus on the negatives. We think about the despair that follows the death of a loved one, but not the wonderful moments spent together celebrating their life. We think of the heartbreak of a relationship ending, but not the exhilaration and freedom of being unattached. We might even scold our loved ones, friends, or coworkers for something minor, when we ourselves wallow in similar negativity. But it is in these moments that gratitude can be used to alter this way of thinking.

Finding positives and accentuating them is the easiest way to turn those proverbial frowns upside down and gray skies back to blue. Try catching someone doing something right for a change, not something wrong. Giving praise for a job well done will lift all parties involved.

Badass Practice

Listening Is an Act of Love and Respect

We don't always have to donate time and energy to other parts of the world. Sometimes, help is needed much closer to home. Is a parent, sibling, spouse, friend, or coworker having a difficult time? Help lift their spirits by letting them experience that loving feeling. Invite them to coffee or dinner, surprise them with a simple gift, or take them somewhere they like. Lean forward and listen closely. Just listen.

Below, list people who might need to be listened to:

DATE

Weekly Objectives:

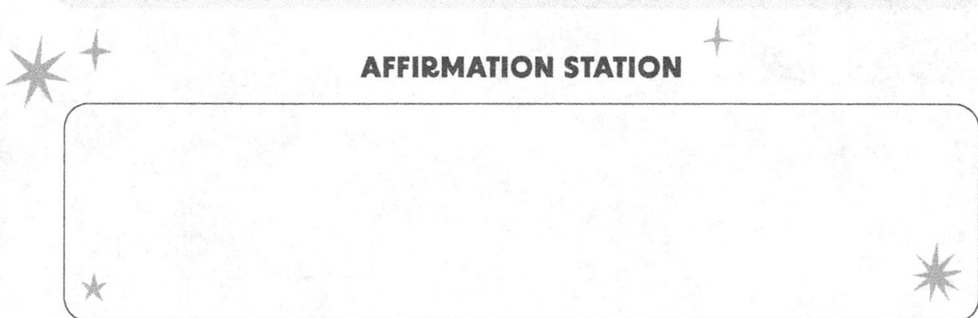

AFFIRMATION STATION

HABIT	MON	TUES	WED	THURS	FRI	SAT	SUN
Drink twelve cups of water							
Move/exercise							
Eat all three meals							
Check in with friends or family							
Sleep well							
Practice hobby/interest							
Reflect on your day							

DATE

Monday

Tuesday

Wednesday

Thursday

Tasks	Date

Friday

Saturday

Sunday

Tasks	Date

Weekly Thoughts and Reflections

Weekly Objectives:

AFFIRMATION STATION

HABIT	MON	TUES	WED	THURS	FRI	SAT	SUN

DATE

Monday

Tuesday

Wednesday

Thursday

Tasks	Date

Friday

Saturday

Sunday

Tasks	Date

Weekly Thoughts and Reflections

DATE

Weekly Objectives:

AFFIRMATION STATION

DATE

Monday

Tuesday

Wednesday

Thursday

Tasks	Date

Friday

Saturday

Sunday

Tasks	Date

Weekly Thoughts and Reflections

DATE

Weekly Objectives:

AFFIRMATION STATION

HABIT	MON	TUES	WED	THURS	FRI	SAT	SUN

DATE

Monday

Tuesday

Wednesday

Thursday

Tasks	Date

Friday

Saturday

Sunday

Tasks	Date

Weekly Thoughts and Reflections

Chapter 11

Gratitude Habits—Reframe Your Life by Seeing the Positive Possibilities

I have been taught the art of reframing by my dearest friend, Nina. She is a true practitioner of gratitude and a living reminder to me of how valuable and truly life changing reframing is.

I'll give you an example: When she was a very young mom, her workaholic husband abandoned the young family. Of course, she was shocked and reeling from this change, but she set about taking care of her daughters and herself and dealt with the considerable financial fallout. Very quickly, she reframed what happened: it was an opportunity to improve her financial literacy and learn how to manage her money. And how true this was! She has bought and sold many houses and created a rocking stock portfolio and a very happy life. When I am with her, I see her gently guide people toward reframing the vicissitudes of life and seeing the positive possibilities. In a world of Debbie Downers, be a Nina.

When we begin a daily practice of recognizing the positive events that occur and the pleasant encounters we have with others, we will start being more thankful as the days pass. Perhaps it's someone who holds the door for you at the supermarket, the animated conversation you have with a stranger while at the coffee shop, or a hug with someone you love. These are the small moments, and often the ones we forget. Savor their beauty and what they tell you about humankind—that we do live among many good people.

Badass Practice

How to Have an Attitude of Gratitude

- **Be grateful** and recognize the things others have done to help you.
- **Say, "Thank you,"** to someone and be specific about what you appreciate and why you appreciate it.
- **Send a handwritten thank-you note.** These are noteworthy because so few of us take the time to write and mail them.
- **Think thoughts of gratitude**—focus on two or three good things that happened today—and notice calm settle through your head, at least for a moment. It activates a part of the brain that floods the body with endorphins, or feel-good hormones.
- **Remember the ways** your life has been made easier or better because of others' efforts. Be aware of and acknowledge the positive things, large and small, going on around you.
- **Keep a gratitude journal** to list the people or things you're grateful for today. The list may start out short, but it will grow as you notice more of the good things around you.
- **Join forces to do good.** If you have survived illness or loss, you may want to reach out to others to help. This is a way of showing gratitude for those who reached out to you.

Below, list one of the seven practices that you will prioritize in the next few days and reflect on its particular importance in your life.

DATE

Weekly Objectives:

AFFIRMATION STATION

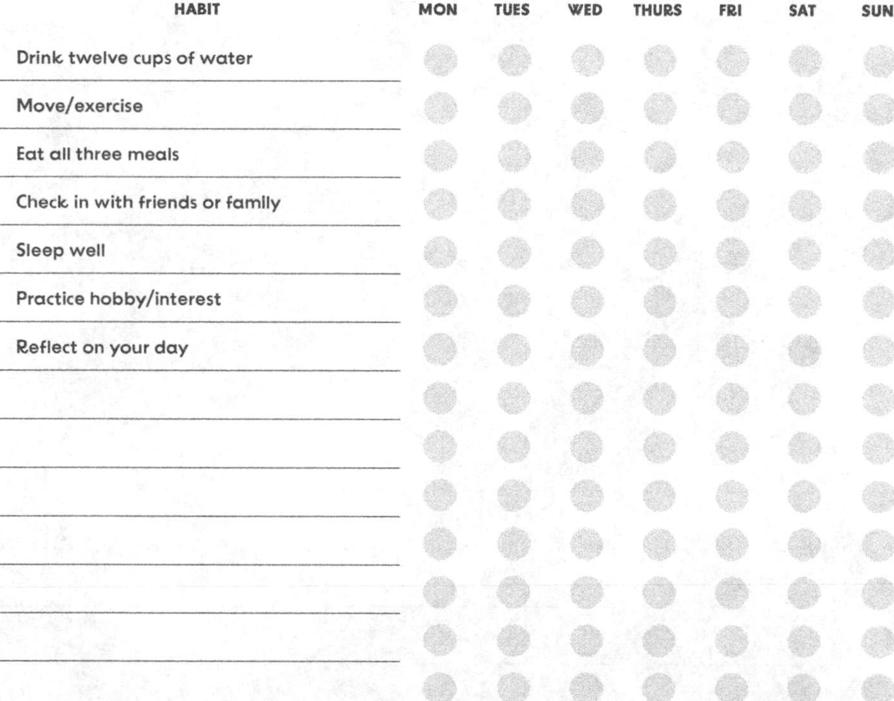

HABIT	MON	TUES	WED	THURS	FRI	SAT	SUN
Drink twelve cups of water							
Move/exercise							
Eat all three meals							
Check in with friends or family							
Sleep well							
Practice hobby/interest							
Reflect on your day							

DATE

Monday

Tuesday

Wednesday

Thursday

Tasks	Date

Friday

Saturday

Sunday

Tasks	Date

Weekly Thoughts and Reflections

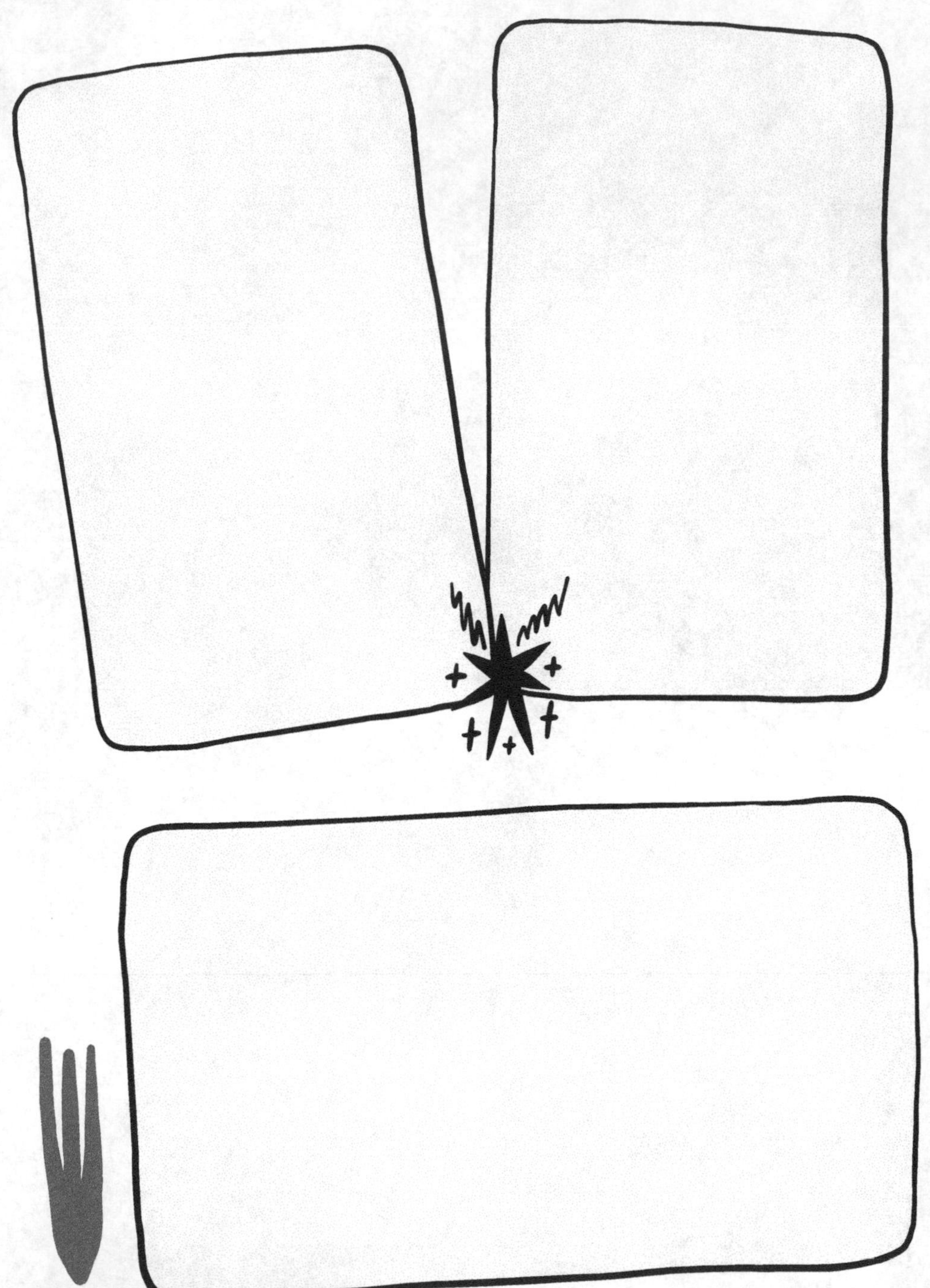

DATE

Weekly Objectives:

AFFIRMATION STATION

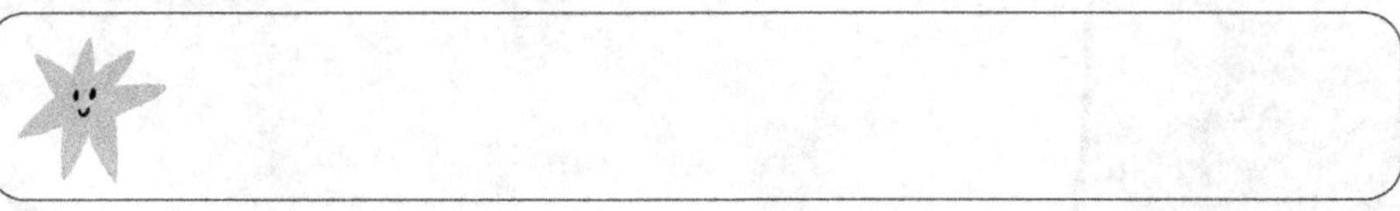

HABIT	MON	TUES	WED	THURS	FRI	SAT	SUN

DATE

Monday

Tuesday

Wednesday

Thursday

Tasks	Date

Friday

Saturday

Sunday

Tasks	Date

Weekly Thoughts and Reflections

DATE

Weekly Objectives:

AFFIRMATION STATION

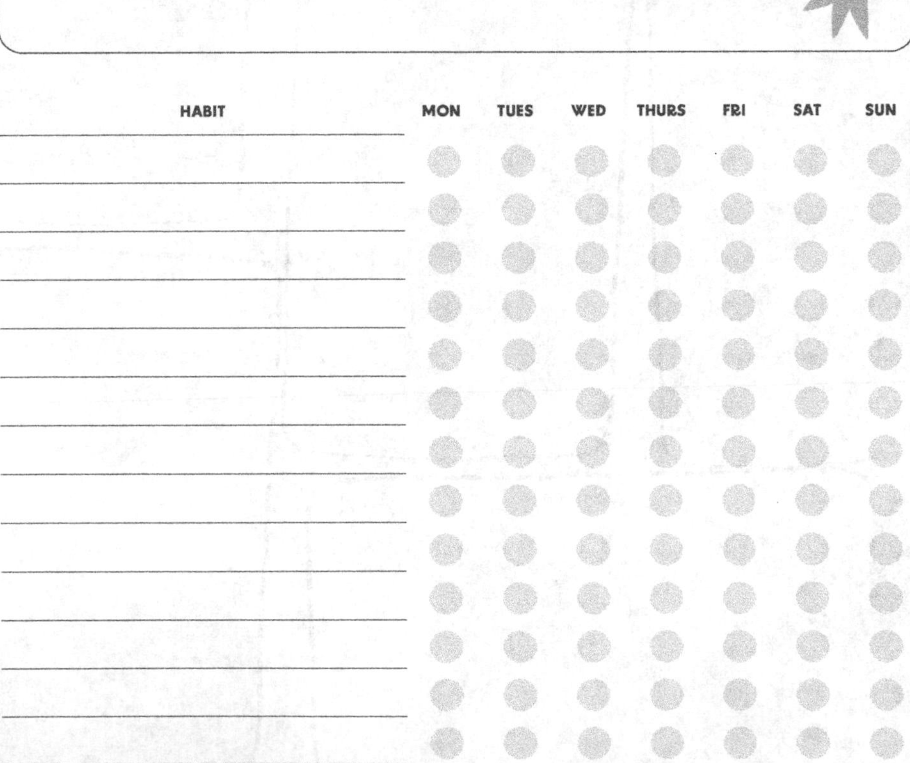

DATE

Monday

Tuesday

Wednesday

Thursday

Tasks	Date

Friday

Saturday

Sunday

Tasks	Date

Weekly Thoughts and Reflections

DATE

Weekly Objectives:

AFFIRMATION STATION

HABIT	MON	TUES	WED	THURS	FRI	SAT	SUN

DATE

Monday

Tuesday

Wednesday

Thursday

Tasks	Date

Friday

Saturday

Sunday

Tasks	Date

Weekly Thoughts and Reflections

Chapter 12

Reflecting on Your Year—And Looking Forward

The last month of this year of reflection is a good time to take stock of your life. Looking back at the year and assessing what worked and what didn't is also an instrumental aspect of your self-development. Looking back is very healthy and a key part of your personal journey.

If something didn't improve your life, calm your mind, feed your soul, or help you get ahead, maybe you need to just let it go. No matter what your spiritual orientation is, for true personal development it is essential to do the inner work. You must explore yourself deeply and discover what is meaningful to you, sense where you need to go, and set your spiritual goals. At the end of the day, at the end of this year, and at the end of your life, it will not matter how many houses or cars you have; what really will count is what kind of person you were and how you treated others.

Look inside and face the following questions. Can you answer them satisfactorily? By doing so, you will be able to determine and change the future course of events. The process of taking stock is an essential step in a life well lived, a life full of soul work, and a life that is challenging but ultimately joyful.

- Was the work of the last year "soul work"?
- Did you express yourself creatively?
- Did you take care of your family? Did you help others?
- What do you really want in your life for the coming year?
- What are your goals for the new year? Your resolutions?
- Who do you want to be?

Badass Practice

Think "Best-Case Scenario" All the Time

Let's face it, these last few years have been really stressful, and just watching the daily news can bring you down. I often remind myself to adjust my attitude through gratitude. One simple way is to think about what you *have* instead of what you lack. Many people overanalyze situations, psych themselves out, and only consider the worst-case scenarios. I, for one, am guilty as charged. Let's start this new year on a positive note and make a list of your "best-case scenarios." What are the best things that could possibly happen to you? To your family? To the world? Have fun with this and think big.

Below, write down some of those best-case scenarios:

As you enter the last month of the year, think about your self-care strategies for the coming year and list your goals, aspirations, inspirations so that the new year is your best year!

DATE

Weekly Objectives:

AFFIRMATION STATION

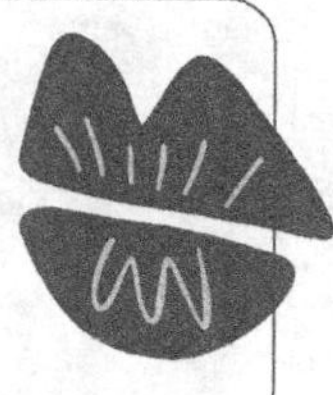

HABIT	MON	TUES	WED	THURS	FRI	SAT	SUN
Drink twelve cups of water							
Move/exercise							
Eat all three meals							
Check in with friends or family							
Sleep well							
Practice hobby/interest							
Reflect on your day							

DATE

Monday

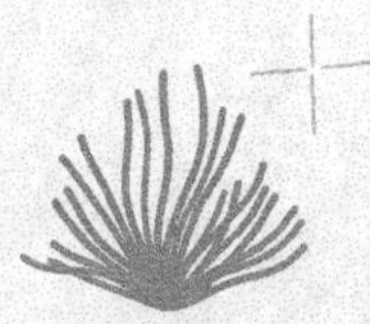

Tuesday

Wednesday

Thursday

Tasks	Date

Friday

Saturday

Sunday

Tasks	Date

Weekly Thoughts and Reflections

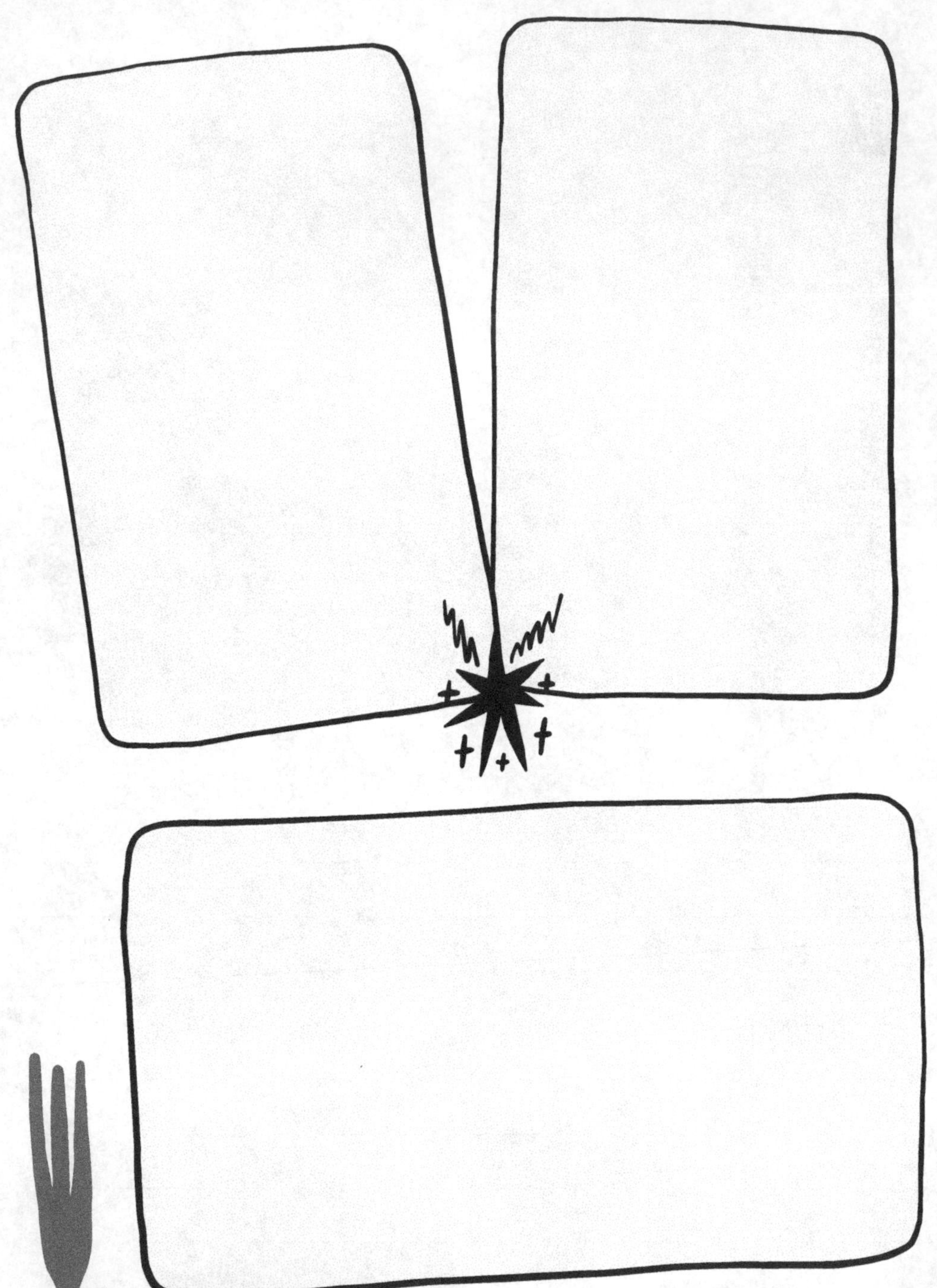

DATE

Weekly Objectives:

AFFIRMATION STATION

HABIT	MON	TUES	WED	THURS	FRI	SAT	SUN

DATE

Monday

Tuesday

Wednesday

Thursday

Tasks	Date

Friday

Saturday

Sunday

Tasks	Date

Weekly Thoughts and Reflections

DATE

Weekly Objectives:

AFFIRMATION STATION

HABIT	MON	TUES	WED	THURS	FRI	SAT	SUN

DATE

Monday

Tuesday

Wednesday

Thursday

Tasks	Date

Friday

Saturday

Sunday

Tasks	Date

Weekly Thoughts and Reflections

DATE

Weekly Objectives:

AFFIRMATION STATION

HABIT	MON	TUES	WED	THURS	FRI	SAT	SUN

DATE

Monday

Tuesday

Wednesday

Thursday

Tasks	Date

Friday

Saturday

Sunday

Tasks	Date

Weekly Thoughts and Reflections

DATE

Weekly Objectives:

AFFIRMATION STATION

HABIT	MON	TUES	WED	THURS	FRI	SAT	SUN

DATE

Monday

Tuesday

Wednesday

Thursday

Tasks	Date

Friday

Saturday

Sunday

Tasks	Date

Weekly Thoughts and Reflections

Afterword

You Can Do All Things, but Maybe You Don't Have To

Dear You,

First off, good job on getting through the year and tracking your life. I sincerely hope you found some of the ideas herein to be helpful and that they helped you sail through your tasks and rock the good self-care you so richly deserve. My hope is also that, in the process of tracking your habits, noting your successes, and reflecting on your days and how you use your time, you have found a few things you no longer need to do. Try editing your life: less is more.

I catch myself all the time doing something that is not going to move any needle or make a difference in my life or anyone else's; it's just not worth the time. Time is the single most valuable resource in your life, so it is incumbent upon all of us to use our precious time well. Give yourself permission to do less, so you can do the things that will make you happy, bring you peace of mind, help you achieve your career and personal goals, and inspire you to embrace and celebrate your true self.

Start a "To Don't" List

My parting homework for you is to make a different kind of list, one that I think will be liberating and invigorating. List down whatever no longer serves you (or becomes what I call a "time vampire") and stop doing it!

In parting, I want to thank *you*. You are a badass and completely awesome. I wish you all the best!

XOXO,

Becca

About the Author

Becca Anderson comes from a long line of preachers and teachers from Ohio and Kentucky. The teacher side of her family led her to become a woman's studies scholar and the author of *The Book of Awesome Women*. An avid collector of meditations, prayers, and blessings, she helps run a "Gratitude and Grace Circle" that meets monthly at homes, churches, and bookstores in the San Francisco Bay Area where she currently resides. Becca credits her spiritual practice of setting intentions and crafting affirmations with helping her recover from cancer and wants to share this with anyone who is facing difficulty in their lives.

- Becca shares her inspirational writings and suggested acts of kindness at thedailyinspoblog.wordpress.com.
- She also blogs about awesome women, sheroes, and boundary-breakers at theblogofawesomewomen.wordpress.com.
- Follow her on Facebook, Pinterest, and on Twitter at @AndersonBecca_ and on Instagram at @BeccaAndersonWriter.

Check Out These Other Badass Books by Becca!

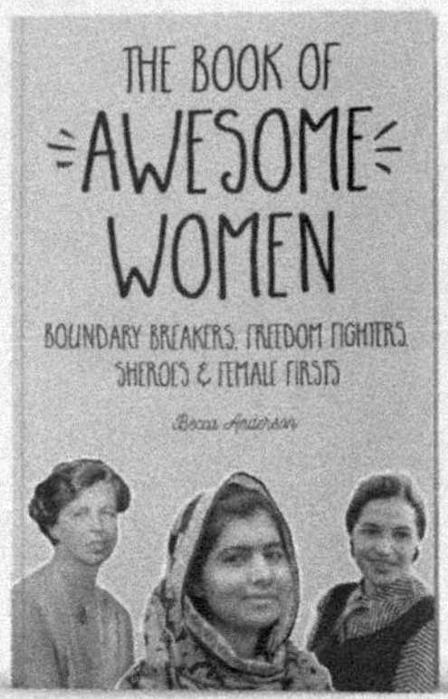

Paperback • $16.95
978-1-63353-583-1
Published 07/25/2017

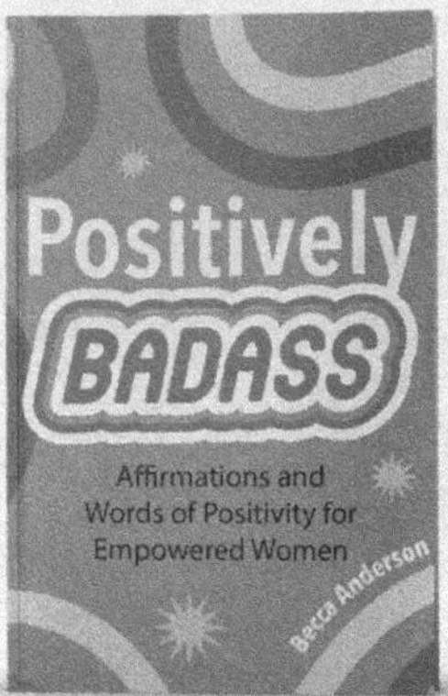

Paperback • $18.95
978-1-68481-001-7
Published 10/11/2022

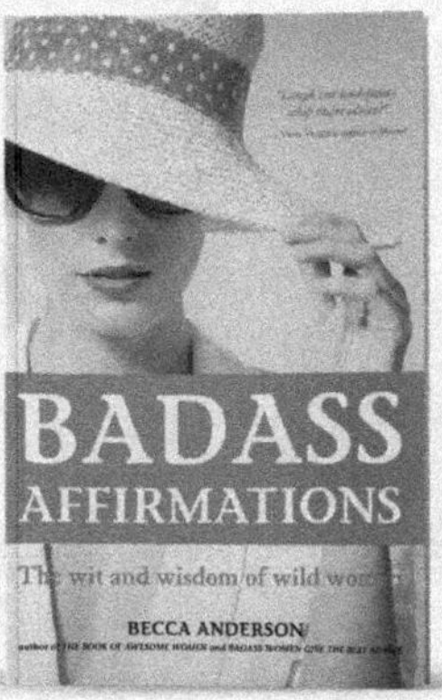

Paperback • $15.99
978-1-63353-752-1
Published 05/15/2018

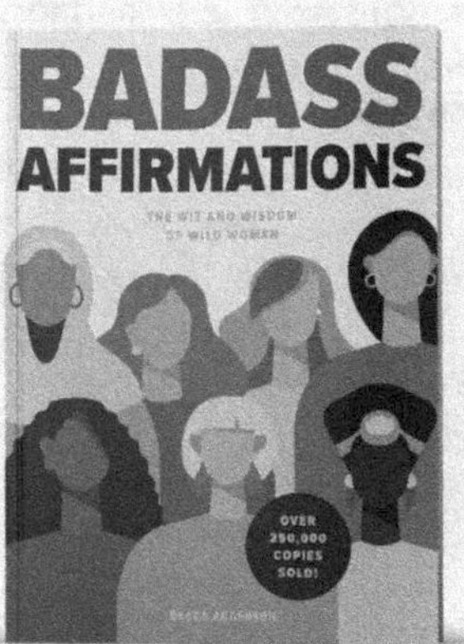

Hard Cover • $29.99
978-1-68481-249-3
Published 3/14/2023

Mango Publishing, established in 2014, publishes an eclectic list of books by diverse authors—both new and established voices—on topics ranging from business, personal growth, women's empowerment, LGBTQ+ studies, health, and spirituality to history, popular culture, time management, decluttering, lifestyle, mental wellness, aging, and sustainable living. We were named 2019 *and* 2020's #1 fastest-growing independent publisher by *Publishers Weekly*. Our success is driven by our main goal, which is to publish high-quality books that will entertain readers as well as make a positive difference in their lives.

Our readers are our most important resource; we value your input, suggestions, and ideas. We'd love to hear from you—after all, we are publishing books for you!

Please stay in touch with us and follow us at:

Facebook: Mango Publishing

Twitter: @MangoPublishing

Instagram: @MangoPublishing

LinkedIn: Mango Publishing

Pinterest: Mango Publishing

Newsletter: mangopublishinggroup.com/newsletter

Join us on Mango's journey to reinvent publishing, one book at a time.

CPSIA information can be obtained
at www.ICGtesting.com
Printed in the USA
LVHW081758140323
741605LV00004B/842